Section 28

Section 28 stops public money from being spent on the schools and elsewhere. Section 28 is not about bullying.

This booklet traces £1 million of public money diverted used to promote gay rights and homosexuality. This rep...... what researchers have uncovered in just three weeks. It is the tip of an iceberg.

There is direct evidence that gay rights projects are taking away money that should properly be spent on education or helping treat sick people (including those with fatal diseases such as cancer, heart disease or AIDS).

What Section 28 of the Local Government Act 1988 requires:

"(1) A local authority shall not-

(a) intentionally promote homosexuality or publish material with the intention of promoting homosexuality;

(b) promote the teaching in any maintained school of the acceptability of homosexuality as a pretended family relationship.

(2) Nothing in subsection (1) above shall be taken to prohibit the doing of anything for the purpose of treating or preventing the spread of disease."[1]

Section 28 should be extended because some health authorities are:

- promoting the most medically dangerous forms of homosexual practice;
- facilitating criminal behaviour between homosexuals;
- engaging in homosexual proselytism.

It should be illegal to promote homosexuality to school children because:

- The great majority of parents think homosexual practice is wrong - *and it is wrong*;
- Manipulating vulnerable young people is not acceptable. They need protection from homosexual proselytism;
- Young people, particularly teenage boys, can go through a phase of experiencing same-sex attraction. This phase should not be exploited;
- The large sums of public money involved are better spent on health care and education;
- There are already enough problems with teenage promiscuity without adding to them. Homosexual behaviour carries high risks to health.

Promote marriage, not homosexuality

The vast majority of ordinary parents want their children to grow up, get a good education, settle down and get married. Their aspiration is that one day their children will have their own families.

Parents believe that education has an important role in teaching young people about the responsibilities of adult life. They believe it is right for the values of the home to be supported by schools.

The evidence from opinion polls confirms that this is precisely what parents want. Well over 70% strongly support promoting marriage in schools.[2,3]

In January 1999 the Government Green Paper on the Family stated that,

> "Marriage is still the surest foundation for raising children and remains the choice of the majority of people in Britain".[4]

In England, the Secretary of State for Education, David Blunkett, has ordered that *non-statutory* guidance issued on Personal and Social Education should include teaching about the importance of marriage.[5,6] But what use will this be if local authorities are allowed to promote homosexuality and homosexual families in schools? It will be a return to what was happening in London schools in the 1980s.

Concern about sexual experimentation

Britain has the highest teenage pregnancy rate in Western Europe.[7] The average age at which young people first had sex fell from 20 to 17 years in the period 1966 to 1991. It continues to fall.[8] There is widespread concern about the breakdown of the family on the upcoming generation.

Most children are still brought up by married parents. Seventy percent of them live in households headed by a married couple. Only 7% live in cohabiting households, but, significantly, 24% live in a lone parent household.[9] Three out of every five of these lone parenthood households were created through divorce or separation.[10]

Today around 25% of children will see their parents divorce by the age of 16.[11] Britain has the second highest divorce rate in Europe.[12]

©Collections/Liz Stares

What has happened to the family is very serious for our society because the family is a primary carrier of values.

If promoting homosexuality in schools is legalised vulnerable children will become even more confused.

It will be the most vulnerable children of all who will be

most affected. A generation of young people have grown up with one parent absent - usually the father. It is well established that this can have a profound effect on young boys. Not surprisingly they can be sexually confused in the teenage years. They can long for the relationship with their father that they never had. They may seek a same-sex relationship to substitute for this.[13] This makes them more easily manipulated by adults who promote the homosexual lifestyle.

A homosexual phase

Even before the recent problems of family breakdown it surely has always been true that young teenage boys can go through a phase of having an attraction for other boys. In most cases this is just a passing phase. But there is concern that such young people could be encouraged to experiment sexually in a way that they will later come to regret. Many will regret it because they know it to be morally wrong and feel guilty. Others will have even greater cause for regret since homosexual activity carries grave risks to health.

The health risks

Male homosexual activity is hazardous. Anal intercourse is particularly dangerous - so dangerous that those who have *ever* engaged in it are banned from giving blood by the UK's National Blood Service.[14] One in six gay men in London are HIV positive according to the Terrence Higgins Trust.[15] Hepatitis B, neisseria gonorrhoea and treponema pallidum are other diseases commonly contracted by homosexuals that can also be fatal.

Young people are not being told the truth about homosexual experimentation. Even leading homosexual researchers have complained that in health promotion materials for homosexuals "death is never mentioned" and "the danger for an uninfected man of having unprotected sex with an infected man is never explicitly stated."[16]

Concern about homosexual proselytism

Instead of promoting marriage in schools the evidence is that some local authorities want to promote homosexuality. Thanks to Section 28 they have not generally done so in schools. But the situation is changing. Because the Government wants to repeal Section 28 local authorities and NHS Trusts are confidently appointing a growing number of homosexual outreach workers for schools and for youth clubs.

There have been many instances where local authority officials have used their powers to block expenditure which would have been illegal under Section 28. But there have also been many occasions where this has not happened and public money has been spent promoting homosexuality.

This study looks at what local authorities and NHS Trusts are doing now. In so doing it sets the scene for a return to the battles of the 1980s if Section 28 is ever repealed. But first a look at the successful impact of Section 28.

Why Section 28 has worked in schools

If anyone can be thanked for making Section 28 so effective it is Derek Hatton, the disgraced Liverpool Councillor. The property scandals involving Liverpool Council in the 1980s led to various "whistle-blowing" provisions being put on the statute book. These greatly strengthened the independence of Council staff from overbearing Councillors intent on breaking the law. [17,18]

General public awareness about Section 28 has also made it much more difficult for Local Education Authorities (LEAs) to promote homosexuality in schools. It only takes one parent to complain to the District Auditor for an investigation to be launched.

The evidence is that these whistle blowing provisions, plus the threat of District Audit investigation and subsequent surcharging of Councillors, have all made Section 28 effective. There can be no doubt that the move over to local management of schools has helped. LEAs have lost the power to retain large proportions of their education budget.

Certainly the groups which campaigned for a legal ban on the promotion of homosexuality in schools have expressed themselves as well pleased with the way Section 28 has worked in practice. Nick Seaton of the *Campaign for Real Education* explains:

> "Before Section 28 came into force we were getting considerable numbers of parents complaining to us about the promotion of homosexuality in schools. After Section 28 it almost disappeared as an issue. If Section 28 were to be repealed it's almost certain that the promotion of homosexuality would become a huge bone of contention between parents and schools."[19]

Stopped by Section 28

The main effect of Section 28 has been as a deterrent. This is accepted even by those who want Section 28 repealed. Writing in 1992, the gay rights activist Peter Tatchell argued that Section 28 had led to "at least 35 instances of self-censorship by local authorities fearful of prosecution".[20]

Since Section 28 came into force in 1988 there have been many instances where it has prevented the promotion of homosexuality. The following are some examples which have become public:

- In May 1988, East Sussex County Council stopped a National Youth Bureau directory from being distributed in its schools on the grounds that it infringed Section 28. The directory included gay and lesbian organisations seeking to recruit teenage volunteers who had 'a positive attitude to their sexuality'.[21]
- An English county council refused an application for financial assistance to purchase equipment and materials to produce a homosexual newsletter which the Council referred to as a "publicity drive".[22]
- Aberdeen County Council received an application from the "Deck Chair Collective" for crèche assistance for a lesbian event in Edinburgh. The Council's convenor refused the application on strong advice from the Council's lawyer.[23] Other "Deck Chair Collective" grant applications also failed with Kyle and Carrick District Council,[24] and Lothian Regional Council.[25]
- On 23 January 1989 the Scottish Homosexual Action Group applied to the City of Edinburgh District Council for financial assistance towards a "Lark in the Park" festival - described as a "lesbian and gay festival of music, poetry and drama." Prior to Section 28 a grant for a similar event had been awarded to the group. But this time the Council was advised by a barrister that such assistance would contravene the new law. The barrister had "difficulty in accepting that the function would not have the result of promoting homosexuality". The Group withdrew their application. In April 1989 they re-submitted their application arguing "it is not our intention in staging this event to seek to encourage people who are not lesbian or gay to become lesbian or gay". The Council's barrister responded: "it is possible to promote homosexuality without converting people to homosexuality... to grant this application would be illegal and *ultra vires*". The Council passed a motion declaring that, in view of the legal opinion, the Council had no alternative but to refuse the grant, but had it not been for the opinion they would have done so.[26]
- In September 1999 Cardiff County Council withdrew funding from the first Cardiff Lesbian and Gay Mardi Gras because of fears about Section 28.[27]

As will be seen below some local authorities have been determined to promote homosexuality even with Section 28 in place. But the law has caused even these authorities to think twice.

The health promotion loophole

Whilst the pro-homosexual activities of Education Departments have been curbed, large amounts of local authority money have still been spent promoting homosexuality. Often this has been done under the guise of health promotion work - which is exempt from Section 28. On top of this, where local authorities cannot act because of the law, NHS health promotion trusts have stepped in.

Section 28 does not prohibit "the doing of anything for the purpose of treating or preventing the spread of disease."[28] This legitimate exception, intended to protect work against sexually transmitted diseases, has been ruthlessly exploited for illegitimate means. (For an examination of expenditure on HIV/AIDS prevention and HIV/AIDS treatment, see Appendix II).

The contention of this publication is that local authorities and health authorities are now funding gay proselytism of young people.

For instance: What *does* health promotion have to do with funding youth workers to target young people who are "questioning their sexuality"?

Why do *so many* publicly funded youth worker posts require no qualifications apart from being homosexual?

What *does* health promotion have to do with telling young people how to commit homosexual acts in public and how to deal with the police if they get arrested?

What *does* health promotion have to do with taking young people to adult 'gay pride' festivals?

What *does* health promotion have to do with funding a web-site to help homosexual men find places to have dangerous, anonymous sex?

What *does* health promotion have to do with producing leaflets giving advice to homosexual holidaymakers on how to ask for sex in five languages, and how to bring pornography and sado-masochist equipment back into the country when they return?[29]

The advert in the *Pink Paper* expressing Enfield & Haringey Health Authority's support for the London Mardi Gras, 1999

The homosexual phase

Young people are vulnerable. The teenage years in particular can be a very confusing time because of the enormous physical and hormonal changes which teenagers go through.

This confusion can be especially acute over the issue of sexual identity. Research shows that some young people, more often boys than girls, go through a phase in their development in which they feel attracted to members of the same sex. Most of those who go through this phase grow out of it. The largest and most recent UK study of sexual behaviour is the national *Sexual Attitudes and Lifestyles* study by Kaye Wellings and her colleagues. This study found that

> "A form of bisexuality prevalent in early adulthood may represent a transitional phase in which preferences are tested through experimentation with different lifestyles and relationships".[30]

Young men (aged 16-24) were more likely to report having been attracted to someone of the same sex than other age groups.[31] According to the study some 2.4% of men and 1.7% of women have had a "homosexual experience" without any genital contact.[32] "Homosexual experience" (which may involve little more than simply putting an arm around another person): "is often a relatively isolated or passing event"[33] or "a transient part of their sexual development."[34]

Even for those who have had actual genital contact "half of all men and two thirds of women who report having had a same-gender partner in their lifetime have had only one."[35] The study states that for them "the experience was a single, possibly youthful and experimental, occurrence and for whom homosexual inclination was not a lasting orientation."[36]

Rejecting the gay lifestyle and its subculture

So the Wellings study finds that even of those young people who engage in homosexual activity, most will come to reject it. This is also confirmed by a very large US study of 36,741 American adolescents aged 12 to 20. It found that 1% reported 'homosexual experience' (this includes non-sexual experience) in the previous year (1.6 % of boys and 0.9% of girls). But of this 1% only 27.1% identified themselves as homosexual or bisexual.[37] The vast majority of those young people who had had homosexual experience rejected a homosexual identity. They do not call themselves "gay".

Many publicly-funded homosexual youth projects focus on "coming out" techniques which force young people to decide whether they want to be thought of as "gay". Why should pressure be put on them to make that choice? The majority of young people who have engaged in homosexual activity do not go on to label themselves as homosexual or bisexual.

Adopting a gay identity separates a young person from the mainstream of society and precludes some of the major satisfactions of adult life. Teaching "coming out" techniques can manipulate young people into making profound choices, the implications of which can be lifelong.

Homosexual conditioning

Most boys who experience same sex attraction never commit homosexual acts. However some do. But even with this group, most try it once or with one person and never again. Only around 40% of those who try out homosexual activity continue with it.[38]

That young people can be influenced by their environment into having homosexual activity is illustrated by the established fact that homosexuality is more prevalent in boarding schools. The Wellings study finds clear evidence that, "Schooling has an important influence on whether someone has ever had a homosexual partner..."[39]. Experience of same-sex genital contact is nearly three times more likely amongst those men who have attended boarding school.[40]

The Wellings researchers therefore accept a *facultative thesis*: because there are more opportunities for same sex contact in boarding schools it happens more often.[41] More opportunity means more likelihood of homosexual experimentation. All this is plain common sense.

The "born that way" argument

In recent years three scientific papers have proposed a "gay gene" theory. All of these have now been soundly rebutted by the wider scientific community. In 1993 Professor Dean Hamer, announced that he had found the "gay gene".[42] Two years later he faced an investigation for misconduct when a member of his own staff who voiced doubts about his work was sacked.[43] In 1999, after a two year study looking at his claims, scientists in Canada concluded that there was no basis for Hamer's conclusions.[44] After the rejection of Hamer's work in *Science* Peter Tatchell, the gay rights activist, said,

©Collections/Michael StMaur Sheil

"I'm amazed that it's taken this long to destroy what is obviously a totally implausible theory. It *is* a choice, and we should be glad it's that way and celebrate it for ourselves."[45]

Identical twins have identical genes. Yet a much-vaunted study by researchers Bailey and Pillard found that only 52% of identical twins in their study were *both* homosexual. In the other 48% of cases one was homosexual and the other heterosexual. If genes determined sexual orientation then each twin would have to have the same sexual orientation (either homosexual or heterosexual).[46] This would mean that Maria Eagle MP, sister of openly lesbian MP, Angela Eagle, would be a lesbian too. But she isn't. And even if she was, the 'gay gene' could only be 'proved' if every set of twins were either both heterosexual or both homosexual.

The fact is that no serious geneticist believes that a single gene can dictate behaviour. Behavioural genetics looks at many genes in combination. Even if a link between genes and behaviour is established, it only indicates a predisposition. No one *has* to behave in a certain way because of their genetic make-up. No one is gay because of their genes.

Homosexual proselytism

Civilised societies have always restrained sexual activity. Until comparatively recently, social control strongly promoted marriage. Homosexual proselytism seeks to reverse this and to manipulate young people into seeing homosexuality as an acceptable and morally right lifestyle.

For most people the biggest obstacle to homosexual conversion ("coming out") is their own conscience. The Wellings study found that 70% of men believe that homosexual practice is wrong.[47] Even younger respondents to the study were "not markedly more tolerant than older ones".[48]

This booklet shows that local authorities and health authorities are softening up young people by promoting homosexuality as acceptable, and homosexual experimentation as legitimate.

Key points

- Most of those who experiment with homosexuality do so once and never again.
- Most young people who have experimented with homosexuality do not see themselves as "gay" and should not be forced to do so.
- More opportunities (such as gay youth groups) will mean more experimentation.
- The idea of a gay gene is, in the words of one leading gay-rights activist, "totally implausible".
- No-one has to behave in a certain way because of their genes.
- Homosexual proselytism seeks to manipulate young people into seeing homosexuality as morally right.
- For most people the biggest obstacle to "coming out" is their own conscience. 70% of men believe homosexual practice is wrong.

Tracking a million

Researchers at The Christian Institute took three weeks to track down £1 million of public money being spent on promoting homosexuality. This is the tip of the iceberg. Researchers looked at job recruitment adverts in back issues of one homosexual newspaper, the *Pink Paper*.[49] They also looked at one grants scheme run by London Councils. During a three week period this information was followed up by obtaining public accounts from local authorities and health authorities, statutory accounts from Companies House and annual returns from the Charity Commission.

The total cost of all the jobs in the survey, advertised in the *Pink Paper* over the year to October 1999, was £685,000. In addition, researchers uncovered £340,000 given to gay and lesbian groups in 1999 by London Councils through the London Boroughs Grants Scheme. One example of an LBG funded organisation is LAGER (Lesbian and Gay Employment Rights). As its name suggests the organisation campaigns for homosexual employment rights. LAGER's turnover for 1997/1998 was £173,963.[50] It received £108,457 from London Boroughs Grants - 62% of its income in that year.[51] (See Appendix I)

Few local authorities came near to giving as much as London Boroughs Grants (LBG), whose money comes from all 33 of the London Authorities.[52] LBG was set up after the abolition of the Greater London Council and its total grants budget is over £28 million and covers more than 500 voluntary groups.[53]

As will be seen the sums involved in promoting homosexuality add up to considerably more than £1 million a year. Nationally the HIV prevention budget comes to £52.3 million annually.[54] Some of this is going to health authority projects which promote homosexuality. This study has only analysed £500,000 of this money, along with another £500,000 taken from council budgets.

(The separate budget for *treating* HIV/AIDS patients comes to £199.3 million.[55] The success of medical *treatments* is compared to the failure of HIV *prevention* in Appendix II.)

Techniques

Local authorities have found ingenious ways to fund the promotion of homosexuality. Like many such groups, MESMAC ("MEn who have Sex with Men: Action in the Community") in the North East of England receives funding from several Council departments all at once. The true scale of Council funding is not clear without tracking down all the streams of public money involved.

If the body being funded is a limited company or a registered charity, then the accounts are in the public domain and filed at Companies House or the Charity Commission. If the body being funded is part of a local authority or health authority, tracking down the funding is a much more complex matter.

How the *Gay Times* covered Manchester Mardi Gras

Islington Council has left much of the promotion of homosexuality in its area to the local Health Authority which is, of course, exempt from Section 28. Camden and Islington NHS Health Promotion Trust fund youth workers to help young people "come out". They also produce teachers' manuals and explicit homosexual sex guides, and publish booklets to help youngsters adopt a homosexual lifestyle.

Homosexual proselytism in Manchester is handled by a range of voluntary organisations funded by the City Council. The 1999/2000 budget includes £17,400 to the Lesbian and Gay Switchboard and £31,200 to the Peer Support Project (PSP) which advises school children on "coming out and staying out".[56] Linked to PSP is "Lesbian and Gay Youth Manchester" which takes children to adult gay pride festivals all over the UK.

Many local councils have set up joint projects with NHS Community Health Trusts. The workers involved are often appointed on the basis of being a homosexual or lesbian. Qualifications are often deemed to be unnecessary.

Key facts from the survey of recruitment adverts will be considered next.

Jobs for the Boys

The Christian Institute surveyed job adverts placed in the *Pink Paper* between May 1998 and October 1999. A total of 73 posts[57] were identified which claimed to:

- Help those who are "unsure of their sexuality"; and/or
- promote safer sex advice for homosexuals; and/or
- provide advocacy for homosexuals; and/or
- provide "support" or youth activities for homosexuals.

All jobs involving direct social care or health care of those suffering with HIV or AIDS were excluded from the survey.

In most cases the advertisements clearly stated the rate of pay, usually as a range depending on qualifications and experience. In the figures below employer's costs ("the on-costs") have been estimated as 20% of the salary.[58]

- 23 of the 73 posts in the survey required applicants to be homosexual.
- 31 of the 73 posts were aimed at youth. 18 of these were for some sort of youth club.

- 40 posts claimed some sort of health aspect. 5 of these were outreach workers needed to attend gay clubs or "public sex environments" ("PSEs").
- 3 advertisements were for posts which involved direct schools work. (London Borough of Haringey, Stockport Borough Council and Newham Community Health Services NHS Trust).
- The total amount spent "up-front" per year on the 20 *local authority* posts in this survey is between £99,479 and £131,486. (In fact, Councils spend much more than this - see below.)
- The total amount spent per year on the 28 *health authority* posts is between £450,021 and £515,279.

It must be remembered that this is not an exhaustive survey of all publicly funded jobs which promote homosexuality. The survey looked at the jobs advertised in only one newspaper. There are many other places where such jobs are advertised. Many of the adverts were for new jobs, but it could also be that a job is advertised to replace a person who is leaving. In any event, the proportion of jobs advertised must be only a fraction of those which are already in existence.

Voluntary organisations

The remaining 25 posts in the survey[59] were with voluntary organisations which get most of their funding from public sources. Our calculations assume that these voluntary organisations receive only 50% of their funding from public sources. In reality the proportion is likely to be much more. One example is *Healthy Gay Manchester*. It advertised for five posts, varying from "Fundraising and Events Co-ordinator" to "Sessional Group Workers". The cost of these posts adds up to at least £49,201.[60] The organisation's web site gives extensive tips on what to do if you are arrested for committing homosexual acts in public.[61] Its Accounts for 1997/98 gave an operating income from six health authorities of £307,950 and voluntary donations of only £9,984.[62] Income from health authorities makes up 83% of Healthy Gay Manchester's total income.

A reasonable estimate for the total annual cost of all the local authority and health authority posts advertised in the *Pink Paper* over an 18 month period is £740,000. Excluding jobs advertised from May to September 1998, jobs advertised in the year period October 1998 to September 1999 would cost £685,000 pa. This comes to £1,025,239 per year when the LBG's £339,825 is added.[63]

One year's worth of gay rights jobs, advertised in one paper, cost the tax-payer
£685,000

Gay lessons

Because of Section 28 local authorities cannot require schools to promote homosexuality. That does not mean they have not tried. Below is a list of examples where attempts have been made to promote homosexuality in schools. Some of the examples constitute clear breaches of Section 28. Others illustrate techniques that some local authorities have successfully used to get around the law.

As the prospect of repealing Section 28 comes closer, some local Councils have become more daring in their promotion of homosexuality, including the appointment of homosexual "outreach workers". The *Gay Times* admitted in February 1999:

> "many local authorities are turning a blind eye to Section 28 and actively encouraging youth projects and other council-funded initiatives not to restrict their activities simply out of fear of breaching the legislation."[64]

Just what some of these initiatives are will now be considered. Some of these examples were uncovered as a result of the jobs survey. Others came to light via different means. The cost to the public purse is given where it is known.

The London Borough of Haringey

In 1988, in the face of considerable public criticism for its promotion of homosexuality, and just as Parliament was about to legislate against the promotion of homosexuality in schools, Haringey reiterated its commitment to putting homosexual issues on the school curriculum.[65] The extent to which this has been implemented is not known. However, it is known that in August 1998 the London Borough of Haringey advertised the post of "Part-time Youth Worker (Lesbian or Bisexual Female)" to work alongside two male workers as part of the Outzone Schoolswork Project. The 18 hours a week post had a salary ranging from £3,000 to £5,270 and was jointly funded by the Enfield and Haringey Health Authority and Barnet NHS Healthcare Trust. The Schoolswork Project, and its sister project the Lesbian, Gay and Bisexual Club, were billed as: "two exciting and unique pilot projects… in Haringey and Barnet schools." The youth work post was to "develop work around sexuality and related issues with schools primarily in Haringey and Barnet." It began with training teachers in secondary schools, before going on to do direct work with schoolchildren. The London Borough of Haringey also runs a lesbian, gay and bisexual homework club.[66]

Stockport

Stockport Metropolitan Borough Council's Education Division advertised three posts for homosexual youth work to help run its Young Gay Men's Project (2 posts) and its Lesbian/Bisexual Project (1 post). The assistant youth worker with the Lesbian/Bisexual Project was required to "assist the Development Worker With Girls and Young

15

Women in continuing to develop a safe, welcoming, educative and supportive environment for Girls and Young Women who are identifying as lesbian or bisexual." The post involved working with schools and colleges and other agencies and preparing leaflets, posters and other visual materials "for distribution to appropriate venues". "Press releases, radio and communications to other agencies" were also part of the brief, as were "sexuality training initiatives".[67]

Newham Community Health Services

Newham Community Health Services NHS Trust fund a "Male Development Worker" for "Gay, Lesbian & Bi-Sexual young people" (salary £19,726 a year). The advertisement for the post required applicants with:

> "...experience of working with young people, in particular those who identify as Gay, Lesbian or Bi-Sexual, and with young men in single sex settings ... confidence in discussing sexual health matters ...[and] facilitating sexual health promotion, education and/or training with young people ... Knowledge of PSHE/education issues".

Although no formal educational requirements were given in the advert, the post did involve,

"development of young people's sexual health services, [including] direct sexual health/promotion with young people in a variety of settings, clinic-based sexual health work, schools, colleges, youth clubs."[68]

'Health Promotion' in Avon

A video encouraging school children as young as 13 to experiment with same sex partners has been produced by Health Promotion Services Avon. It aims to "explore ways in which sexuality can be included in the curriculum."[69] Scenarios in which pupils are required to imagine themselves include:

> "Michael is 15 and his boyfriend wants him to have sex. He really wants to but he is nervous. Michael knows he should use a condom but doesn't know where to go for help. What should he do? Consider: ...What might you do?"[70]

Other characters they are asked to act out include: "Married man who was 'done' for cottaging... S & M heterosexual woman... Transvestite cabaret artist".[71] "Cottaging" is slang term for homosexual sex in public lavatories. S & M is short for sado-masochistic. These terms are defined in the teacher's handbook so that pupils can understand.

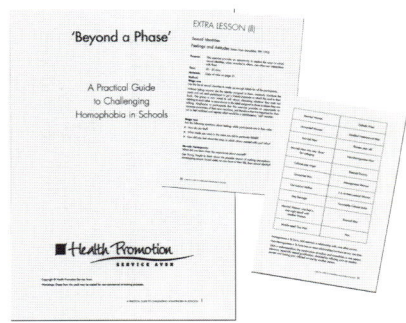

It is also suggested in the guide that teachers should ask pupils, "If your sexuality was known about, would you be able to: ... Adopt a child? ... Marry your partner? ... Have sex legally at 16? ... Have the sex you want when you want it? ... Expect positive role models at school?"[72] Amongst the "skills" which the teaching pack seeks to give to children are the ability to "cope with 'coming out' and questioning one's sexuality" and "making positive sexual choices".[73]

The video is a powerful recruitment tool. It particularly targets "Young People questioning their sexuality".[74] Almost all of the young people interviewed in the video are well-versed in pro-homosexual arguments. A young lesbian is one of the main characters in the video. She recounts a promiscuous search for satisfaction with boys before turning to same-sex relationships. She describes her mother as "very religious" and a "homophobe"[75].

Towards the end of the 15 minute video, intended for children 13 years old and above, one of the young people, 'Karl', suggests that children should "try experimenting with other boys and girls and see who you feel most comfortable with."[76]

Camden and Islington NHS Trust

In 1996 dozens of primary and secondary schools received a 160-page guide produced by the Camden and Islington NHS Trust telling teachers how to create "positive" images of homosexuals and persuade children that homosexuality is an acceptable lifestyle.[77] This guide was called "Colours of the Rainbow". Although it was produced by the Health Promotion Service of the Trust, at a reported cost of £40,000,[78] it clearly has little to do with health. Rather, it is designed to be a homosexual proselytism handbook for teachers of children aged 5 to 16. In three forty-five minute lessons for five year-olds called "Spectrum of Sexuality" the teacher is instructed to explain various scenarios to his pupils: "Michael is 6, has black hair, green eyes, white skin and is about the same height as... (point to a pupil). He likes sweets and lives with his two mums, Mona and Yasmin. Ask the class to draw/paint his family. Name and label them."[79] Two other families are similarly described. One who has a mother and a father and the other who has two fathers.

In a lesson for seven year olds, pupils are given pictures of an all-female group and an all-male group. The purpose of the lesson is to discuss the use of "ambiguous sexuality images and sexual imagery in advertising". The men are close together in suggestive poses wearing only shorts. A pair of women in the sexily dressed female group are holding hands. The children are asked to describe how the pictures make them feel.[80] For a lesson intended for fourteen year olds, teachers are provided with information from the homosexual campaign group Stonewall about "homophobic violence". Teachers are encouraged to give the pupils information about joining Stonewall.[81]

Birmingham City Council

In 1998 Birmingham City Council, in partnership with the Birmingham Health Authority, produced 80,000 copies of a 150-page information book for the youth of the city. Free to children aged between 14 and 17, the guide was made available on request to teachers and youth workers for distribution to those in their charge.[82] It cost £84,000 in printing alone.[83] Staff costs and other overheads will mean the actual cost was substantially more than this. The *Young People's Guide* covers many areas: alcohol; death; eating disorders; racism; and stress, in each case giving information on where to get advice and support. It stresses at the beginning "You do not need your parents' permission to contact any Helping Service. Parents will not be told."[84]

The guide tells young people to beware of prejudice, claiming that 'anti-gay' prejudice "is often based on fear and ignorance".[85] The book suggests that "Meeting and talking with other people who are lesbian, gay or bisexual is important in order to feel good about ourselves."[86]

For those questioning their sexuality and perhaps wishing to hear a view other than a pro-homosexual one, there is nothing in the *Young People's Guide*. There are nine pages of solid homosexual proselytising material with extensive tips on "coming out". It ends the section with quotes from five young people aged 15 to 19, three of whom are homosexual, and one who "wasn't sure" (and by implication now is sure) about her sexuality.[87]

Save for one section on smoking (which strictly advises youngsters to stop) the guide is unusually sloppy in the advice it gives to young people. In the section on HIV/sexually transmitted infections it blithely states that "They are as common as colds or flu" and "They are just part of life".[88] The very next page states "Sexually transmitted infections are not like colds. They don't just go away if left."[89]

Islington Council

The name of Islington has been synonymous with the use of public money to promote homosexuality since the 1980s and the radical policies of the former Greater London Council.

The Borough Library service produced a booklet called "Strength and Pride" - the "Islington Libraries guide to books, music, videos and information". The 52-page guide covers homosexual books, magazines, videos and music for homosexuals. Shelf references are included along with the usual list of gay helplines.[90]

Most of the videos in the guide are described with reference to their sexual content. The literature is not much better. Of 105 books listed 54 are stocked by Islington Libraries. "Spartacus" is a gay tourism guide (shelved at 647.947). "The Lesbian Sex Book" covers "anonymous sex and much more" (shelved at 612.6).[91]

Even Islington Libraries have stopped short of stocking all the titles they recommend. Perhaps if Section 28 was repealed they would buy them in. Recommended in the guide but absent from the shelves are four titles which promote homosexuality as a pretended family relationship. In the section of the guide called "Issues for Parents/Carers/Children and Young Adults" we are told about "The generous Jefferson Bartleby Jones" - "the story of a boy with 'two Dads' who loans them to friends! Special times and family life with gay parents; in Jeff's case he shows it's double the fun!" "Daddy's roommate" is a "Child's perspective on life with Daddy and Frank. Positive images of everyday life for children with gay parents: simple text, superb illustrations." There are two other similar titles in this section. [92]

Also absent from the shelves but recommended is "Out of Bounds" - "a romantic and touching novel showing the forbidden love of a school teacher for one of his pupils and of the many hazards therein. Set in the idyllic surroundings of an English boys school, the love blossoms around the cricket field…"[93]

Youth workers & outreach workers

As well as sending homosexual workers into schools, some publicly-funded projects target young people through homosexual youth work.

Tower Hamlets

The London Borough of Tower Hamlets advertised the post of "Temporary Youth Worker-in-charge" at PHASE, "Tower Hamlets' Lesbian, Gay and Bi-Sexual Youth Project", at a salary of £12,397 p.a. PHASE is for young people (under-25) "questioning their sexuality and/or gender" or who identify themselves as homosexual.[94] It aims to be "a relaxed, supportive and friendly environment."

Tower Hamlets also advertised in April 1999 for 10 temporary youth workers for the PHASE project.[95] The adverts specified that each of the ten youth workers and the youth worker-in-charge must have had "experience of working with young people aged 9-25 years". The job description does indeed specify that the youth worker post was designed to meet the social and development needs of children aged nine and above.[96] According to the Area Youth Co-ordinator at Tower Hamlets, although four suitable candidates were found, none of these ten temporary positions were filled because of funding problems.[98]

PHASE is a very appropriate name for this project since many young people do go through a phase of being attracted to someone of their own sex. In almost all cases they grow out of it and go on to develop normal heterosexual relationships. This project targets *them*.

Manchester City Council

Manchester City Council gives £31,190[99] to the *Peer Support Project (PSP) which exists* "To relieve the mental and emotional crises experienced by young persons who are lesbian, gay or bisexual or in doubt of their sexuality..."[100] The Peer Support web-site itself provides information on "coming out"[101] and PSP publishes "Coming Out and Staying Out" which gives advice to young people about telling their parents they are gay. There is also a section on "safer sex" involving gratuitous use of expletives.[102] The PSP web-site hosts youth groups in the Manchester area such as "Lesbian & Gay Youth Manchester" which meets in the Manchester Lesbian & Gay Centre. Their activities include taking young people on visits to Pride Festivals all around the UK.

PSP produces a newsletter and runs a "Study Club" which aims to provide "extended learning opportunities to Lesbian, Gay and Bisexual young people." These take two forms: "1) Curriculum support 2) Personal & Social Education".[103] Curriculum support is carried out by volunteer teachers who are qualified teachers or currently undergoing training. Personal & Social Education is facilitated by "trained young people from the PSP and other volunteers such as youth workers". Issues addressed include "Sexual health education; Lesbian, Gay and Bisexual culture and history; Challenging/coping with homophobia; Coming out."[104]

Oxfordshire County Council

Oxfordshire County Council's Youth Service is a part of its Education Department. The Youth Service runs a project called "Way

Other Youth Work

The London Borough of Camden's Youth Service advertised in August 1998, for the post of "Gay Male Youth Worker" to organise and deliver a "social education programme". The cost of this part time post was £1,353 a year for 3 hours a week. The purpose of the job was to work with young people to build a gay or bisexual male identity. The applicant himself "should positively identify as Gay or Bisexual".[110]

The London Borough of Newham has three youth work posts as part of its project to develop new and existing youth work with lesbians, gay men and bisexuals aged between 16 and 25. The project has a regular drop-in centre. Recruitment adverts required applicants who would "work towards the social education, political and recreational needs, and individual development of young lesbians, bisexuals and gay men." Two of the three advertised posts required a homosexual. The total salary cost of the three posts came to over £10,000.[111]

The London Borough of Harrow advertised for a "Youth and Community Worker: Working with Gay and Bisexual Young Men (Health)" at a salary of over £18,000 a year. Brent[112], Greenwich,[113] and Hounslow[114] Councils also advertised for youth workers to work with homosexuals. Hampshire County Council advertised for two posts working with lesbian, gay bisexual young people aged between 16 and 25 years.[115] Hammersmith and Fulham advertised for someone to work with young, gay and bisexual men who would "promote a positive sense of self worth – empowering the young men with a comprehensive programme of social, health and personal education."[116] The salaries for these part-time posts ranged from £830 to £3,730 a year. In the case of Brent, the post was full-time with a salary of £17,000, for which the Council has received funding from the Brent & Harrow Health Authority.[117]

Out" which "counteracts the negative conditioning and labelling often associated with gay sexuality in mainstream services and culture".[105] The Way Out group was set up in Oxford in 1996 with only five young people from the city attending. By January 1997 there were twenty core group members. The group is open to anyone under the age of 26 who is either "unsure of their sexual identity" or is lesbian, gay or bisexual. The youth group venue is intended to provide a space to meet "in the explicit intention of excluding the damaging effects of homophobia and heterosexism". [106]

A second Way Out group has been started in Banbury. Oxfordshire County Council Youth Service advertised in the *Pink Paper* for a part-time youth worker working several hours a week to support the development of this second group.[107] Previous experience of working with homosexual young people in a youth work setting and having an understanding of homophobia is deemed 'essential' for the new Banbury group. Qualifications, however, are desirable but not essential.[108]

All workers with the Way Out groups are briefed to "ensure the young people are making informed decisions in their sexual behaviour and relationships". The job description for the advertised post requires the new youth worker to "build appropriate relationships with young people and assist in providing non-formal educational opportunities for young people in the Lesbian, Gay and Bisexual Youth Group." [109]

Manchester's bi-annual gay festival - It's Queer Up North

Gay jamborees

Every year now publicly funded gay festivals are taking place in some of the major cities of England and Scotland. Manchester City Council has designated £100,370 for homosexual groups in 1999/2000, £12,000 of which is for *It's Queer Up North*, which its organisers describe as an "arts festival".[118] In fact, the 1996 programme reveals that many of the performance events are suggestive, explicit or even pornographic in nature. The 1996 festival offered acts such as "The Go Girls" performing "Passionight" ("lesbian courtship... the heights of erotic fantasy")[119], along with dozens of homosexual films and performers such as Britain's "first internationally successful porn star."[120]

Manchester City Council also supported the 1996 and the 1998 Manchester Mardi Gras. In 1998, in what gay press described as an "unprecedented move", Manchester City Council appointed Ian Wilmott, a local gay

Two of this summer's gay festivals as reported by the *Gay Times*

rights activist, as Event Co-ordinator to oversee the organisation of the Mardi Gras festival.[121] *Gay Times* commented that "Mardi Gras cannot take place without Council backing".[122]

Another example of major public funding of a gay festival is Glasgow's Glasgay! The 1998 festival included live performances such as "The Dyke and The Porn Star", described as a "sexually explicit drama about a young butch dyke's obsession with a femme top porn star,"[123] and "Night Sullied Flesh" - "sexually explicit, uncompromising - and not for the faint-hearted."[124] Gala Ltd, the company that organises and runs Glasgay! festivals, received a total of £28,200 of public funds (two-thirds from Glasgow City Council) towards the costs of the 1998 festival[125] representing 71% of the total income.[126]

Pretended families

Section 28 specifically prohibits local authorities from promoting homosexual relationships as a "pretended family".

Rights of Women (ROW) is a London-based organisation which gives legal advice to women on a variety of issues such as family law and employment rights. ROW has five staff members, one of whom specialises in lesbian parenting. Their annual report boasts examples of their advocacy of lesbian parenting, including the publication of a legal handbook for lesbian mothers. The 1986 edition of ROW's legal handbook argues that "more mums are more fun"[127] and includes a section on adoption and fostering and a comprehensive guide to artificial insemination - complete with contact details for an organisation that will assist with sperm donors.[128] 94% of Rights of Women's £100,026 budget comes from London Boroughs Grants - the body which distributes grants on behalf of all the London local authorities.[129] The Lesbian Mother's Legal Handbook is a long and bitter attack on traditional families. Public libraries in Cambridge[130] and Southampton[131] and Milton Keynes[132] all stock this book at public expense.

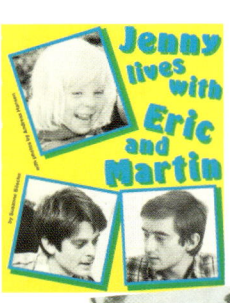

Public money also pays for the promotion of lesbian parenting in Leicester. The Leicester Lesbian, Gay and Bisexual Centre – "the biggest of it's kind in the country" – is funded by local councils to the tune of £35,385 from Leicester City Council, Leicestershire County Council and Rutland County Council, along with £8,528 from Leicestershire Health Authority. In 1997/98, public funds constituted 39% of its £113,874 income. [133]

The centre runs a programme on the third Sunday of every month known as the "Lesbian Parenting Group". Meetings include "information sharing about donors, legislation and the practicalities of parenting - in general and specific to our situations." There is also a "Lesbians making Babies" workshop organised by two members of the group.[134]

Under Section 28 it would be illegal for a local authority to advocate that schools teach children about self-insemination techniques for lesbians. But since self-insemination is not illegal for girls at any age, repealing Section 28 would remove the main obstacle to it being promoted in schools by local authorities.

'Books for children'

One strategy for promoting the acceptability of homosexual families has been the production of children's books depicting homosexual parenting as normal. The most infamous of these is Jenny lives with Eric and Martin.[135] This book, which is still stocked in Hertfordshire Public Libraries,[136] shows two homosexual men living together, one of whom has a child called Jenny from a previous relationship. It describes simple details of daily life to show the "normality" of the little girl's home situation. This includes breakfast in bed with her father (who appears to be naked) and his homosexual lover.

Neal Cavalier-Smith is the publisher who co-launched Prowler Press (a gay pornography company) and who now owns the rights to Jenny lives with Eric and Martin. Mr Cavalier-Smith is also a Director of Stonewall, the gay rights group. In a recent interview with *Gay Times* he observed,

> "The thing that defines gay men is gay sex. Our aim is to make people feel good about gay sex, and by so doing, to make the world a better place for gay men."

Referring to Jenny lives with Eric and Martin, he went on to boast,

> "When Section 28 is successfully repealed, as I believe it will be shortly, we will be rushing to republish an updated version of the book and we shall make sure that every school which wants a copy will get a copy."[137]

Other books have been produced more recently in the United States with the same aim of presenting homosexual parenting to children in a positive light. Zack's Story, stocked in Gloucestershire County Libraries,[138] is a particularly lavish example, illustrated with full colour photographs of a boy named Zack, his mother, and her lesbian lover.[139]

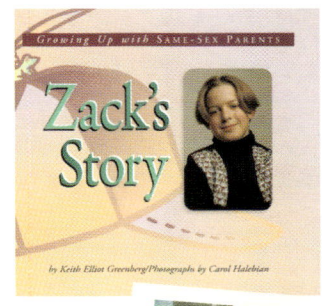

Scenes from Jenny lives with Eric and Martin

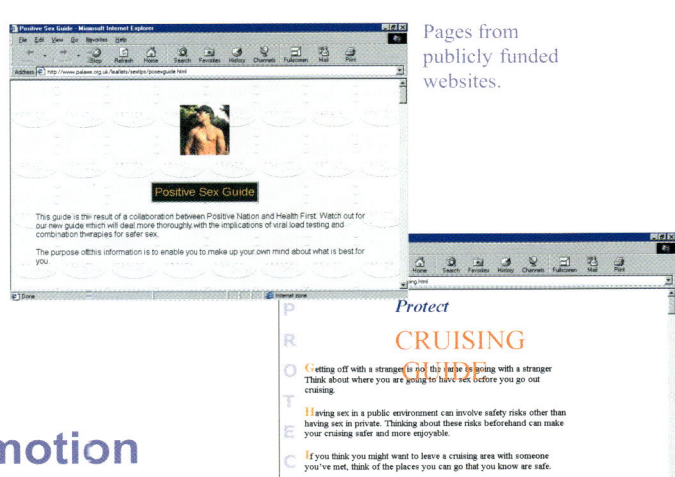

Pages from publicly funded websites.

Health Promotion

Lambeth, Southwark & Lewisham Health Authority

In 1997/98 the Department of Health's ring-fenced HIV prevention allocation to Lambeth, Southwark & Lewisham Health Authority amounted to £1,750,000.[140] Voluntary sector contracts with organisations working with homosexual and bisexual men cost £847,562[141] - equivalent to 48% of that allocation. One of the many projects funded was the development of the Pleasure Palace Website. Its primary audience is HIV positive men.[142] It is therefore surprising to find that it includes a step-by-step guide as to how to engage in sex in public places (known as "cruising", or, if it takes place in toilets, "cottaging"), and what to do if you get arrested for doing so.[143]

Lambeth, Southwark & Lewisham Health Authority and Merton Sutton & Wandsworth Health Authority together gave £229,500 in 1997/98 to the *Healthy Gay Living Centre*.[144] In September 1999 the centre advertised four posts as part of its NRG group.[145] According to an information leaflet NRG is a "fun group for lesbian, bisexual and gay people under 25 in South East London ... an alternative to the commercial gay scene." The group allows people to "meet, socialise and make new friends". Staff are all homosexual. NRG is not all "serious discussions and advice ... The aim of the group is to socialise and have fun, so we have pizza and video nights, trips out to the cinema, residentials, pool, food, and good conversation." The group provides a service for homosexuals and "those questioning their sexuality." It is working "towards the empowerment of young lesbians, bisexuals and gay men, and to build self-confidence and self-esteem."[146]

Newcastle City Council

Newcastle City Council funds a full-time post at MESMAC North-east. MESMAC is short for "MEn who have Sex with Men: Action in the Community". The post was advertised as a "Community Worker (Young gay & bisexual men)". The salary was

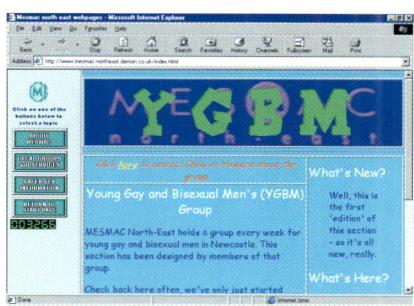

£12,912. No formal qualifications were required but the applicants needed "experience of working with gay communities and networks."[147] MESMAC runs a helpline and gives out a range of health information. It is also funded by other local Councils and by the local Health Authority.

The MESMAC website gives information about its work with 16 to 25 year olds - the Young Gay and Bisexual Men's Group (YGBM). It emphasises that MESMAC "provides a safe place to meet other young gay and bisexual men". The website provides detailed information on techniques of encouraging young people to declare they are a homosexual (to "come out"). It goes on to explain how the leaders of the youth group "operate a two-week rule, in that those who attend are not allowed to 'make a move' on new members of the group within their first two weeks, allowing people to settle into the group first".[148] Should a homosexual be arrested for committing homosexual acts in public the web-site gives details of local solicitors used to dealing with "cottaging" and "cruising" offences.[149]

Metro Centre

Greenwich's Metro Centre calls itself "A Centre in South East London for lesbian, gay and bisexual people and those questioning their sexuality." It has an openly political agenda. Its Annual Report for 1997/98 commences with reference to "gains in the wider political and social landscape [which] have not yet eventuated - such as an equal age of consent and employment rights wins in Europe".[150] The group claims to be a leading provider of services for young people and its "mini pages" leaflet emphasises that it provides these services for under 16s at various locations, including the Metro Centre itself. The same leaflet gives explicit details about the use of condoms for different sexual practices says that they "hope that whatever you get up to with whoever you are with, is a happy time".[151]

Core services provided by the Centre include "outreach" work - giving condoms and lubricant to patrons at various homosexual bars and clubs. 17,363 condoms were distributed in the year 1997/98, along with 10,142 packs of lubricant.[152] "Safer-sex supplies by post" were also provided.[153] The Report declares that, "In line with Metro Centre policy all services are delivered by

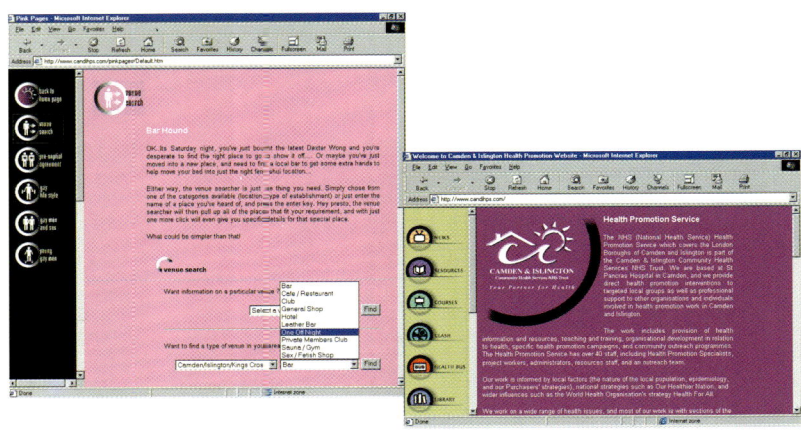

lesbian, gay or bisexual people"[154] As at September 1998 the Centre had 11 staff and 45 volunteers providing these services.[155]

Funding from Health Authorities makes up the vast majority of the Metro Centre's funding. In the accounts for the year ended 31 March 1998 Bexley & Greenwich Health Authority is listed as giving £199,900 in grants. Lambeth, Southwark and Lewisham Health Authority gave a further £10 200. The Social Services and Policy & Resources departments of the London Borough of Greenwich gave £67,251. Together these grants made up 98.7% of the centre's funding. The accounts show a surplus of £8,895. This is in addition to the previous year's surplus of £43,859.[156]

The Metro Centre "aims to work with self-identified lesbian/gay/bisexual people and those who cannot express their sexuality due to homophobia and heterosexism".[157]

Camden and Islington

The Camden and Islington Health Promotion Service clearly has a strong emphasis on homosexual issues. Their internet web-site makes no secret of this. "Gay Men's Work" is one of the six subject headings on the front page of the site and there is a whole section devoted to homosexuals under the heading "Pink Pages".[158]

Top of the list of services in the Pink Pages is "Barhound" - a venue search. Clearly the Trust's definition of 'health promotion' extends to helping homosexual men find places to have sex. The site contains a database of homosexual venues in the London area and provides addresses and directions for each one. The site allows you to pick an area of London and the type of venue you are looking for. The list of 'venues' includes sex shops, fetish shops, hotels, bars (including 'leather' bars), gyms and saunas. Saunas are one of the places where homosexual men often go for casual sex. As "The Ultimate Gay Guide" explains,

"Gay saunas are similar to cruising grounds in two respects. You go there to have sex, and you go there to have sex with no strings attached. The difference with a sauna, compared to a cruising ground is the fact that there is no risk element. Gone are the 'is he or isn't he?' doubts that you may have been thinking on Hampstead Heath or some such place. It's definite. He is."[159]

According to this guide, in one of the saunas recommended by the Camden & Islington website (called Pleasuredrome Central),

> "There is a sign on the wall by the sauna stating that public sex in Great Britain is illegal, etc. (yawn!) but this is obviously ignored. Don't fall into the trap of sitting around thinking that no one is going to break the law."[160]

Pacific 33 is also recommended by Camden Health Promotion Service. The Ultimate Gay Guide describes this as

> "A particularly busy little sauna situated close to North London University (and all the students!) with plenty of darkened cruising areas around the venue."[161]

Saunas are amongst the places where homosexual men are most likely to engage in unprotected sex and thereby place themselves at risk of contracting HIV or another sexually transmitted diseases. Project SIGMA, the gay research group at Portsmouth University, have carried out a detailed study of gay saunas. They found that,

> "Like most places that are used for sexual activity, the saunas we studied depend upon a series of areas and activities each one having a duplicitous purpose relating both to its legitimate function as part of a leisure club and its illegitimate function as a sex club… Gay men who use backrooms, saunas, cruising areas or cottages engage in increased levels of [unprotected anal intercourse]."[162]

It seems extraordinary, perhaps even callous, that a Health Authority should provide a quite extravagant internet service to deliberately facilitate the very activity that places these men at risk. The site also contains very explicit "sex advice", complete with pornographic photographs of homosexual acts between men.[163]

GMFA

Gay Men Fighting AIDS (GMFA) is what could be called a 'radical' HIV/AIDS prevention group.

There are some things that are difficult to describe in words. GMFA's website is one of those things. Their web-site address is not listed in the footnotes here because, of all the materials we have had to review for this publication, GMFA's site is the worst. From the front page onwards and without warning the site features pornographic photographs depicting activities which most people will have never imagined could take place between men. The site is sex-obsessed and gratuitously so. Every activity is described in great detail. The only restraint suggested is the use of condoms. Nothing else, including sado-masochism, is out of bounds.

Courses run by GMFA are advertised in such terms as: "Skills for Gay Life. The whole gay thing - Sorted. By the end of this course you will be: more comfortable with the scene; confident about cruising [searching for sex in public places]; able to ask for the sex you want… GMFA workshops are FREE OF CHARGE."[164] "Bondage for beginners" and "Cruising skills" are other courses run by GMFA.[165]

The British Board of Film Classification (BBFC) argued that a sex education video produced by GMFA breached both the 18 and R18 pornography video guidelines. It could only be released after cuts were made and then only as an 18 pornography video.[169]

To the year ending 31 March 1998, Gay Men Fighting AIDS had a total income of £498,692. Only £6,792 of this came from

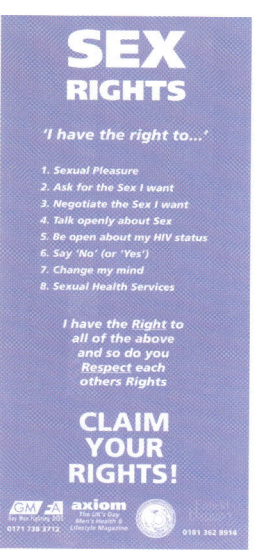

Other projects

Southern Birmingham Community Health NHS Trust recently advertised five posts for its Men's Sexual Health Project working with homosexual men. The salaries alone cost £90,000[170]. Bromley Health Authority advertised for a Gay Bisexual Men's Health Adviser (£17,200) working in the "commercial gay scene".[171] South Buckinghamshire NHS Trust sought a "Gay Men's Community Support Worker" on £11,272 in order to develop support networks and interest groups.[172]

Cornwall and the Isles of Scilly Health Authority advertised for an "out" man to work as a "Part-time Community Worker" for £3,809 a year.[173]

Lothian Primary Healthcare NHS Trust advertised for the post of "Gay Men's Sexual Health Development Worker" as part of it's Harm Reduction Team, developing peer group support for men who have sex with men. Cost £17,120.[174]

Nottingham Community Health NHS Trust's GAI Project advertised for Gay/Bi Men's Sessional Outreach Workers to join a "small friendly team working to promote the health of gay and bisexual men on the commercial scene or in cottaging/cruising sites." Each part time post carries a salary of just under £1,000 per year.[175]

donations. £466,427 (94%) came from "contracts" i.e. work paid for by other bodies.[166] One of these projects is the Hampstead Heath project. GMFA advertised for a worker for this project explaining: "Hampstead Heath is Europe's busiest cruising area. GMFA have been providing men who use it with information and condoms & lube since 1993... Shifts are from 9 or 10pm till 3 or 4am." This contract is worth £75,671 to GMFA.[167]

GMFA's accounts do not indicate the sources of their income. However it has been possible to establish that, in the year 1997/98, Kensington & Chelsea and Westminster Health Authority gave £26,000 to GMFA for "AIDS prevention"[168]. In the same year Lambeth, Southwark & Lewisham Health Authority gave £30,000.

How much all of this contributes to HIV prevention must be seriously questioned.

Bullying

Homosexual rights groups are lobbying hard for the repeal of Section 28. They claim that Section 28 is a "bigots charter"[176] which prevents schools from countering 'homophobia' and stopping the bullying of homosexual pupils. Sir Ian McKellen, writing to Stonewall supporters, alleges that,

> "Homophobic bullying and abuse are going unchallenged in British schools. Young people who identify as lesbian or gay are still growing up feeling alone, without information, guidance or support. Section 28 intimidates teachers who want to help - and gives others the excuse to ignore homophobia".[177]

Specific instances are cited by Stonewall where they claim that Section 28 has caused bullying and even terrorism and the deaths of homosexuals:

> "The brutal attack on schoolboy James Hudson is just one reason why we MUST repeal Section 28 now." [178]

> "..the government must repeal Section 28. It may end with bombs, but it begins with bullies in the playgrounds."[179]

Bullying in schools

All bullying is wrong. Children are taunted by other children because of their physical appearance, a disability, their height, their home background. Some are picked on for being intelligent.

There is never any justification for bullying. It must be dealt with firmly by schools no matter what type of bullying it is. There is a serious problem of bullying in many schools. This is primarily related to a lack of consistent discipline and order in schools.

Bullies and Victims in Schools by Valerie Besag is generally considered to be a classic study of bullying in schools. Besag quotes one 1986 study of 4000 children, which found that,

> "38 per cent had been bullied by other children badly enough to describe the experience as terrifying. Of the sample, 8 per cent of the boys and 2 per cent of the girls had found the experience to have had a chronic and severe effect on their everyday lives." [180]

A February 1999 survey by NOP Research Group found that:

> "more than four out of ten (43 per cent) children aged between 7 and 16 years in Britain say that they have been bullied at some time."[181]

Studies on 'homophobic bullying'

Researchers from the London Institute of Education, who argue that there is a serious problem of 'homophobic bullying', admitted in November 1997 that:

> "To date there has been no systematic survey of the experiences of young lesbian, gay men and bisexuals in relation to homophobic bullying (or hate crimes)." [182]

This is still the case. The studies that do exist are qualitative and focus on the attitudes and experiences of a small, unrepresentative samples of pupils.[183, 184] The London Institute of Education teachers survey (quoted above) was commissioned and paid for by Stonewall and the Terrence Higgins Trust. Both are campaigning pro-homosexual groups. The title of the report was *Playing it Safe*. The researchers admit that there was a low response rate (31%) to their survey of schools.[185] Stonewall reported the research they had paid for in these terms :

> "82% [of teachers] were aware of verbal homophobic bullying and

abuse, and 26% said they were aware of physical bullying which was motivated by homophobia".[186]

The questionnaire asked about instances of "general verbal and physical bullying" in school.[187] What teachers describe as name-calling is redefined as "homophobic bullying" by the researchers. The report clearly states on the first page that:

> "For the sake of brevity, throughout the remainder of this report, incidents of verbal and physical bullying where terms such as lesbian, gay, queer or lezzie have been used will be referred to as homophobic bullying. Where findings relate only to verbal incidents or only to physical incidents this will be stated."[188]

So the 82% of teachers who were "aware of homophobic bullying" were actually those who had ever heard pupils abuse one another using the words "lesbian, gay, queer or lezzie". Such words are used by children as terms of abuse along with such words as "spastic", "divvy", "fatso", "swot", "moron" and sexually rude words. Children can be cruel and they use words that they think will hurt. That the researchers have discovered that "lesbian, gay, queer or lezzie" are particularly popular terms of abuse, sadly, should surprise no one. That these cruel children also hit other children whilst using these terms of abuse is also no surprise.

The researchers quote a definition of homophobia as,

> "an irrational fear and dislike of individuals who identify as lesbian, gay or bisexual. This fear usually results in judgemental, discriminatory and aggressive acts of hatred."[189]

But what the researchers have completely failed to prove is that *any* of the children on the receiving end of the abuse were actually "individuals who identify as lesbian, gay or bisexual". Some of them may have been. But that is not what the study shows. All the researchers have uncovered is that teachers have heard children using slang words for "homosexual" as a term of abuse. It does not prove rampant "homophobic bullying". In fact the comments from some of the respondents make this clear:

> "More often that not, the word, say, queer or lez or whatever is used against a pupil, not because of their sexuality but because the other pupils perceive that as being a form or verbal abuse, so it isn't necessarily related to the pupils' sexuality or perceived sexuality, it's more just a general term."[190]

It is therefore dishonest for gay rights campaigners to use this study to argue that homophobic bullying is rife.

The number of pupils who identify themselves as "gay" in the first place is actually minuscule. This must be so. Even amongst the adult male population only 0.3% of men report having had exclusively male sexual partners[191] and not all of this 0.3% will call themselves "gay". Certainly only a fraction would have been conscious of same-sex attraction whilst they were in school. This further illustrates why it is exceedingly difficult to study the bullying of openly homosexual schoolchildren.

Summary

Even though the number of schoolchildren who are bullied for actually being homosexual is very small, the main point is this: bullying is wrong and should be dealt with in the same way no matter who the victim is. It is grossly unprofessional for a teacher to ignore the bullying of any pupil. This is a straightforward matter of what constitutes professional conduct. Good teachers stop bullies. Section 28 is simply irrelevant to the issue.

An oppressed minority?

It is often argued by gay rights campaigners that Section 28 oppresses gay people and promotes intolerance. Just how oppressed are homosexuals in modern society? Being an oppressed minority is generally considered to involve four factors: poverty; unemployment; powerlessness; and social exclusion.

Certainly homosexuals are in a minority. The *General Household Survey* found that only 0.1% of households are headed by a same sex couple.[192] The *Sexual Attitudes and Lifestyles* study found that 1.1% of men (one in 90) had a "homosexual partner" in the previous year with 0.7% having *exclusively* homosexual partners in the previous year. Over a lifetime, only 0.3% had exclusively homosexual partners.[193] But what about the four indicators of oppression?

Poverty and unemployment?

There is little evidence that homosexuals are particularly prone to poverty and unemployment. Quite the reverse. Active homosexuals are generally well-educated, high earning and over-represented in social class I. They have high disposable income and rarely have any dependants.

Amongst the general population aged 25 to 69, 14% held a degree in 1997 according to the Government's *Social Trends*.[194] SIGMA's Gay Sex Survey in the same year found that 39.7% of the gay men in the survey had "been educated to degree level or higher. These men are more highly educated than the adult male population".[195]

When it comes to employment, a 1994 UK survey of 1,788 lesbians and male homosexuals found that lesbians earn on average £3,000 more per year than heterosexual women.[96]

American surveys confirm the British data about social class and high educational qualifications. In 1988 Simmons Market Research Bureau carried out a readership survey of 8 homosexual newspapers and magazines in the USA. It found that 59.6% had degrees compared with 18% of the general population. In addition 49% were in managerial occupations as opposed to 16% in the general population.[197]

Many market research groups in the US have reported higher than average income for homosexuals. The obvious point that homosexuals rarely have dependants makes a big impact on *per-capita* income. The 1988 Simmons Survey found that homosexuals had treble the per-capita income of the general population ($36,800 compared to $12,287).[198] Since this study was published some major American companies have adopted niche marketing in order to appeal more to homosexuals and their increased spending power.

Studies by the gay research organisation *Overlooked Opinions* have found that the average income for a male homosexual *household* was $55,400 compared to $36,500 for an American median income family household.[199] It is highly significant that this very study is being used by the American Civil Liberties Union to argue for adoption rights for homosexuals.[200]

Business Week reported in 1994 that "gay consumers are five times as likely to earn more than $100,000 a year" as the general working population.[201]

American and British companies would not be targeting a niche gay market year after year unless they made money from it. Clearly they believe that homosexuals are significantly over-represented amongst those with high disposable income.

Powerlessness and social exclusion?

In the United Kingdom, leaving aside Peter Mandelson, there are two Cabinet members and six other MPs who are openly homosexual. All political parties have openly homosexual members. All three main party leaders support the reduction in the age of homosexual consent to 16.

Gay rights campaigners have exercised remarkable political power in recent years. It was only thirty years ago that homosexual acts in private were decriminalised for those aged 21 or over. In 1994 the age of consent was reduced to 18. Soon gay rights campaigners believe it will 16 and the Government has promised to take the draconian step of invoking the Parliament Acts to force the legislation through the House of Lords.

Popular soap operas on television routinely feature homosexual characters who are portrayed as people of high integrity. Popular culture both high and low has examples of successful and prominent homosexuals. There are openly homosexual journalists such as John Nicholson (BBC Breakfast News) and Matthew Parris (*The Times*). In the world of entertainment there are individuals such as Sir Nigel Hawthorne, Sir Ian McKellen, Sir Elton John, and Michael Barrymore. Many of these figures are popular with the public. This does not mean that the public approves of their homosexual lifestyle, but simply that they appreciate their talent.

There is special provision for homosexuals on the media including regular homosexual theme nights on television and other specific programming for homosexuals. The BBC and the Independent Television Commission also have regulations banning broadcasters from causing offence to homosexuals.[202]

In the courts it seems that rarely a week goes by without some new legal precedent being set by gay rights campaigners. Recently the President of the Family Division of the High Court, Dame Elizabeth Butler-Sloss, even called for homosexuals to be able to adopt children.[203]

Far from being an oppressed minority, homosexuals are amongst a successful and favoured elite exercising influence out of all proportion to their numbers. Homosexuals are not socially excluded. John Ruach, an openly gay writer from the United States has questioned the gay orthodoxy which says that homosexual people are an oppressed class. Writing in *The New Republic*, Ruach argued as follows:

> "The standard political model sees homosexuals as an oppressed minority who must fight for their liberation through political action. But that model's usefulness is drawing to a close. It is ceasing to serve the interests of ordinary gay people, who ought to be disengaging from it, even drop it... As more and more homosexuals come out of hiding, the reality of gay economic and political and educational achievement becomes more evident. And as this happens, gay people who insist they are oppressed will increasingly, and not always unfairly, come off as yuppie whiners, "victims" with $50,000 incomes and vacations in Europe. They may feel they are oppressed, but they will have a harder and harder time convincing the public."[204]

Conclusion

One million pounds

- This booklet shows how, in just three weeks, researchers uncovered £1 million of public money being used to promote homosexuality.

- Half of this came from local councils, the other half from health authorities. This is the tip of the iceberg.

Protecting young people

- Section 28 has protected schools over the last eleven years, but now some local authorities are appointing homosexual schools workers to target pupils who are "unsure of their sexuality".

- Homosexual youth workers are also being appointed to promote homosexuality and help young people to "come out". In some cases the aim is to work with children as young as nine.

- The largest publisher of homosexual literature has announced that, if Section 28 is repealed, there will be a major reprint of Jenny lives with Eric and Martin - the notorious book which promotes pretended homosexual families.

- Surveys that claim to show rampant 'homophobic' bullying in schools show nothing of the sort. It may be that in one survey 82% of teachers had heard a pupil call another "gay" or "lezzie" but this constitutes childish cruelty in the same way that children use other derogatory terms to insult one another. It does not constitute homophobic bullying.

- It is unthinkable that any professional teacher should think twice about intervening to prevent bullying when they are made aware of it. Section 28 is irrelevant to the issue of bullying. It is a red-herring to disguise the fact that repealing Section 28 is actually all about using public money to promote homosexuality. And as this booklet shows, it is a great deal of money.

"Health promotion"

- Section 28 does not apply to work on health promotion and this loophole has been ruthlessly exploited to fund homosexual proselytism and extravagant homosexual jamborees.

- Work on "health promotion" has been taken to such an extreme that it is now common practice for staff funded by health authorities to skulk around public lavatories and "cruising" grounds (such as public parks) handing out condoms to homosexual men.

- The definition of health promotion has been stretched to mean promoting criminal and unhealthy behaviour by Camden & Islington NHS Health Promotion Trust. The Trust provides an internet site for homosexuals who want to find the addresses of venues where illegal sexual acts can be committed. The database is fully searchable for maximum convenience.

Parents Rights

- Repealing Section 28 means that homosexuality will once again be promoted in our schools as it was in the time of the Greater London Council in the 1980s. The state has no business in promoting homosexuality to vulnerable young people who can so easily be manipulated. It is profoundly wrong for the values of the home to be trampled on - which will undoubtedly happen in many areas of the country if Section 28 is repealed.

- The promotion of homosexuality in state schools would also be a flagrant breach of the European Convention on Human Rights which guarantees the right of parents to have their children educated in accordance with their beliefs. Should Section 28 be repealed, parents will have to take legal action against local authorities which seek to promote homosexuality in their children's schools. They will need to fight for the right to have their children excused from all lessons where homosexuality is promoted.

It is wrong for public money to be spent on gay rights and homosexual hedonism when it could be spent on education or health care. It is imperative that Section 28 remains and is strengthened so as to include health authorities.

Appendix I : London Boroughs Grants

According to its 1999 directory, the following groups were all awarded public funding by London Boroughs Grants.[205]

Organisation	Amount (£)
Lesbian and Gay Employment Rights (LAGER)	108,457
GALOP [A homosexual group working to influence policing policies]	41,512
Gay and Lesbian Legal Advice	15,368
London Friend [A homosexual advice service]	19,482
London Lesbian and Gay Switchboard	4,078
PACE [A homosexual advice and education service]	54,492
Stonewall Housing Association [A homosexual housing group]*	67,859
Rights of Women [Has a special interest in lesbian parenting]*	88,644
London Lesbian Line	25,521
Total:	**425,413**

*The figure of £339,825 used in the text is arrived at by ignoring Stonewall Housing Association and assuming that only one fifth of Rights of Women's total budget involves gay rights.

Appendix II : AIDS

All of the health posts referred to in this publication concerned HIV/AIDS *prevention*. Health Authority posts distinguish between *prevention* and actual *treatment*.

From the date that AIDS was first diagnosed to March 1999 there were 37,820 individuals diagnosed with HIV in the UK. (HIV is the virus that leads to AIDS). Of these, 60% acquired HIV through homosexual intercourse with a man, and 9% through injecting drug use. Infection through heterosexual intercourse made up 22% of the total but almost invariably this involved exposure to a 'high risk partner'. Only 372 of the total of 37,820 cases of HIV diagnosed so far were acquired through heterosexual intercourse where there was no evidence of a 'high risk' partner or of infection contracted outside Europe.[206]

Everyone now accepts that AIDS is primarily a disease affecting male homosexuals and others in high risk groups such as injecting drug users.

The success of medical treatment

AIDS is a fatal condition which develops from HIV infection. Just under half of those currently infected with HIV have AIDS[207] but, thanks to medical advances, people with AIDS and those with HIV are living longer. According to the Public Health Laboratory Service (PHLS) there have been "substantial falls in the number of AIDS diagnoses" after the peak in 1994/95.[208] The onset of AIDS is being held back much longer because of new medical treatments.

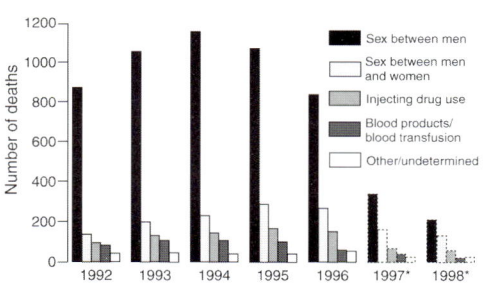

Figure 1 Deaths in HIV infected individuals by year of death and exposure category: UK data to end of June 1999

* numbers, particularly for recent years will rise as further reports are received

AIDS deaths reached a peak in 1994 with 1679 deaths in that year. Although the figures for 1997 and 1998 will rise as further reports for that time period are received, the PHLS is confident that 80% of cases have already been reported. There were 444 AIDS deaths reported in 1998. If this represents 80% of the real total, this would put the likely maximum number for 1998 at 555, less than one third of the death figure four years earlier.[209]

Deaths 1998 England and Wales[210]

Diseases of the Circulatory system (E.g. Heart attacks, strokes)	225,811
Cancers	136,289
Diabetes	5,923
Parkinson's Disease	2,705
Stomach Ulcers	3,909
Asthma	1,350
AIDS	555*

*outside estimate using Public Health Laboratory data that the 444 currently reported represents at least 80% of likely total cases.

The AIDS Treatment Budget

A study reported in the *Journal of Public Policy* in 1994 by Craven, Taghavi and Stewart concluded that compared to spending on other fatal diseases AIDS expenditure had been "extraordinarily generous".[211]

	AIDS	Heart Disease
Health Education & Research	£160 million	£9.9 million
Deaths	553	197,721
Expenditure per death	£289,753	£60

Average cost per case treatment	AIDS	Coronary Artery Bypass Graft	Terminal Cancer
	£11,00 to £51,000	£5,000	£3,500

Source : Quoted by Craven et al[212]

Craven, Stewart and Taghavi comment that,

> "Currently in Britain Regional Health Authorities are spending tens of times more on each patient with AIDS and thousands of times more on each AIDS death than on those with heart disease and cancer... In no other area of health service medicine is there so high a ratio of health workers to patients."[213]

The study found that some Regional Health Authorities had "been allocated so much money that the District Health Authorities cannot spend it all and in attempting to do so have reported schemes inviting ridicule".[214]

The failure of HIV prevention

Researchers from project SIGMA have found that homosexual men, in full knowledge of the risks, and of safer sex practices, continue to engage in risky i.e. "unprotected" homosexual practices. These practices put them in danger of contracting HIV and other potentially fatal infections. A three year study of homosexual men in ten UK cities found that 30% had changed their patterns of risk behaviours with no net benefit: 15% increased their risk and 15% decreased their risk.[215] This position of no aggregate change was also confirmed by another SIGMA study into HIV risk behaviour among gay men who attended "Gay Pride" festivals from 1993-1995.[216]

SIGMA concluded that "non-use of condoms is not because of a lack of knowledge about HIV".[217] After the three years of the study they stated:

> "More men are having sex now than were at the start of the study: this may be a sign that they are more comfortable with sex and less afraid of the risks of sex. This has coincided with the more pro-sex stance of safer sex campaigns aimed at gay men".[218]

Most disturbing of all has been SIGMA's consistent finding that *even men who are HIV positive* continue to engage in unprotected anal intercourse (UAI). The 1997 Gay Men's Sex Survey involving a national sample of 4,307 men recruited at six homosexual events in the summer of 1997 found that overall 28% had engaged in UAI during the past year. But such high risk activity was "more common among men who had tested positive (37%)... than among men who had never tested (21%)" for HIV.[219] The corresponding survey in 1998 found that 43.2% of HIV positive homosexual men in the study engaged in UAI.[220]

Peter Keogh and his colleagues from SIGMA are particularly critical of some HIV prevention work:

> "Gay men can be supported to feel good about themselves as gay men; however, support alone does not help gay men practice safer sex. Instead, gay men should be appealed to as individuals first, individuals who every day make sexual choices in the management of their personal risk."[221]

Ignorance of safer sex practices is clearly not the problem. The Terrence Higgins Trust introduced a new campaign in July 1997 explicitly stating that the campaign's messages,

> "do not seek to deliver any specific safer sex information, which is now well known to gay and bisexual men."[222]

Huge sums of public money are being funnelled into projects claiming the need to provide more and more 'safer sex' information. The effect of much of this material is simply to glamorise homosexual sex. It clearly does little to change the risk-taking behaviour of homosexual men.

References

1. Section 28 of the Local Government Act 1988 added a new section 2A to the Local Government Act 1986
2. A Gallup poll asked a cross section of 660 people "Should children be taught in schools that marriage is a good thing?". 75% said Yes, and 19% saying No. See *Corporal Punishment Poll,* 12 November 1996, Gallup.
3. When *Audience Selection* in a telephone poll asked "Should the teaching of moral values in schools centre on marriage and traditional family values?" 73% said Yes and 21% No. *Nightline Poll Education*, 31 October 1996, Audience Selection. A poll of 506 parents of school aged children.
4. Supporting Families (Green Paper), The Home Office, 1998, Introduction paragraph 8
5. See *The Times* 7 September 1999; *The Daily Telegraph* 7 September 1999
6. *Department for Education and Employment*, Press Release 402/99, 9 September 1999
7. Hansard, The House of Commons, 8 March 1999, Column 36
8. Wellings, K et al, *Sexual Behaviour in Britain*, Penguin 1994, page 38 The median age at which young people first have sexual intercourse has fallen from 20 years for those men aged 55-59 in 1990/1991 to 17 years for those aged 16-34 in the same year. Since the average quoted is a median, this means that half of all men aged 16-34 will have had intercourse by the age of 17.
9. See figures from the General Household Survey quoted in Hansard : The House of Commons : 19 November 1998 (Part 2) col 859 (wa) Percentage of dependent children living in families within private households according to the de facto marital status of the head of family, 1996, Great Britain
10. Loc cit
11. Haskey J, *Children who experience divorce in their family*, Population Trends (87) Spring 1997 ONS, page 9
12. Crude divorce rate. Cited in Ditch J, *A Synthesis of National Family Policies 1996* European Observatory on National Family Policies, Commission of the European Communities, 1998 page 13
13. See the discussion in Satinover J, *Homosexuality and the politics of truth*, Baker Books, 1996, page 104-108. As a psychiatrist he argues that the evidence is unequivocal from eighty studies.
14. National Blood Service, London and the South East, Form FRM/SEZ/BT/006/01 17 November 1997
15. See Terrence Higgins Trust advertisement in *Positive Nation* October 1999, page 25
16. Keogh P et al *Gay men and HIV : Community Responses and Personal Risks* Journal of Psychology and Human Sexuality, Vol 10, No 3/4, 1998, page 70
17. Under the Local Government Finance Act 1988 s.114 the Chief Financial Officer of an authority has a similar duty to make a report to the Council whenever the authority, a committee, sub-committee, joint committee, or any officer has made or is about to make a decision which involves or would involve illegal expenditure, or an illegal action resulting in loss to the authority. Under ss. 115 and 116 the report of the Chief Financial Officer must be considered by the council and until this has occurred the action in question is suspended and the authority are not permitted to enter into any new agreement which would involve incurring expenditure. This last measure is a very draconian power.
18. Under the Local Government and Housing Act 1989, s. 5, the monitoring officer has a duty to make a report to the whole Council if it appears to him that the authority are about to take or have taken an action contrary to the law. The report must be considered by the Council and until this has occurred the course of action in question is suspended.
19. Personal communication with the authors.
20. Tatchell P *Europe in the Pink,* GMP, 1992, page 99
21. Colvin, M *Section 28 - A practical guide to the law and its implications*, National Council for Civil Liberties, 1989, page 5
22. Thomas, P and Costigan, R, *Promoting Homosexuality - Section 28 of the Local Government Act 1988*, Cardiff Law School, 1990, page 28. This Council requested Thomas and Costigan not to disclose its identity in their report into local authority responses to Section 28.
23. Loc cit
24. Ibid, page 29
25. Loc cit.
26. Ibid, page 29-30
27. Stonewall Magazine, Volume 8, Issue 2, October 1999
28. The Local Government Act 1988, s.28.
29. Such a leaflet was produced by Terrence Higgins Trust which in 1998/1999 had an income of £5 million; £818,500 came from twelve Health Authorities. A forthcoming report from the Christian Institute will highlight similar publications and projects done in the name of HIV prevention.
30. Wellings, K et al, *Sexual Behaviour in Britain*, Penguin 1994, page 204
31. *Ibid,* page 195
32. Johnson A M, Wellings K et al, *Sexual Attitudes and Lifestyles*, Blackwell Scientific Publications, 1994, page 204
33. Wellings, K et al, *Op cit*, page 203
34. Johnson A M, Wellings K et al *Op Cit*, page 204
35. Wellings K et al, *Op Cit*, page 213
36. *Ibid* page 214
37. Remafedi G *Demography of Sexual Orientation in Adolescents* in Pediatrics Vol. 89 No 4 April 1992 pages 714 - 721
38. See the estimate based on the Wellings study in Bainbridge et al *Homosexuality and Young People,* The Christian Institute, 1998, page 28
39. Wellings K et al, *Op Cit,* page 209
40. Johnson A M, Wellings K et al *Op Cit*, page 206
41. Wellings K et al *Op Cit*, pages 204, 206
42. Hamer DH, Hu S, Magnuson VL, Hu N, Pattatucci AM, *A linkage between DNA markers on the X chromosome and male sexual orientation* Science Jul 16 1993 (261(5119)):321-7
43. *The Times* 10 July 1995
44. Rice G, Anderson C, Risch N, and Ebers G *Male Homosexuality: Absence of Linkage to Microsatellite Markers at Xq28 Science* Apr 23 1999 (284(5414)): 665-667. See also http://news.bbc.co.uk/hi/english/sci/tech/newsid_325000/325979.stm
45. *The Observer* 25 April 1999
46. A fuller discussion of this is found in Bainbridge I et al *Homosexuality and Young People,* The Christian Institute, 1998, page 6-8
47. Johnson A M, Wellings K et al *Op Cit*, pages 241
48. Loc cit
49. The advertisements had been collated before the project began by a volunteer. Some job specifications were also available.
50. Lesbian and Gay Employment Rights Limited, *Financial Statements for the year ended 31 March 1998* page 3
51. *Ibid,* page 7
52. Details in fax communication from Ian Redding, London Boroughs Grants, 26 October 1999
53. London Boroughs Grants *Directory of funded organisations* January 1999
54. Hansard, House of Commons, 8 February 1999, col 116
55. Loc cit
56. Social and Urban Strategy Committee, Report of the Chief Executive, 15 March 1999, Manchester City Council
57. Four of the posts were excluded from the calculations since they are funded by London Borough Grants - see Appendix 1
58. It is generally accepted that in addition to paying the salary, the actual cost of employing a member of staff, the 'on-costs' are an additional 20%. Employer's national insurance is over half this amount; other costs would include an element for administration costs, accommodation, stationery and telephone. The on-costs could be much more than 20% if there was pension

provision as is common in the NHS and local authorities. The first £4335.01 per year (the lower earnings limit - LEL) is not subject to employer's national insurance. Thereafter the employer pays 12.2% of all earnings above this level. See *Non-contracted out contributions for employers, 6 April 1999 to 5 April 2000*, April 1999, Inland Revenue, page 5. Reducing the on-costs to 7.8% for those 27 posts below the LEL reduces the £1,025,239 by at most £15,000. It is arguable that the 20% on-costs figure should still apply in any case.

59 Four of the posts were excluded from the calculations since they are funded by London Boroughs Grants - considered separately
60 *Pink Paper* 30 April 1999 and 4 June 1999
61 See http://www.hgm.org.uk/page.asp?word=law
62 Healthy Gay Manchester *Accounts for the period ended 31st March 1998*, page 6, note 2
63 The total given by LBG is at least £425,413. This figure is arrived at by ignoring Stonewall Housing Association and assuming that only one fifth of Rights of Women's total budget involves gay rights - see Appendix 1.
64 *Gay Times* February 1999, page 41
65 Haringey Council Education Service, *Equal Opportunities - The Lesbian and Gay Perspective*, page 2. (This document is a summary of *Mirrors round the Walls - respecting diversity"*, the first report of the Curriculum Working Party on lesbian and gay issues in education, received by the Education Committee on 28 March 1988.)
66 *Pink Paper*, 14 August 1993
67 Metropolitan Borough of Stockport Education Division, Job Description for Youth Worker with Young Women who are Lesbian or Bisexual
68 *Pink Paper* 19 February 1999.
69 Health Promotions Service Avon, *'Beyond a Phase': A Practical Guide to Challenging Homophobia in Schools*, February 1999, page 5
70 *Ibid*, page 26
71 *Ibid*, page 31
72 *Ibid*, pages 27-28
73 *Ibid*, page 7
74 *Ibid*, page 6
75 Health Promotions Service Avon, *'Beyond a Phase': A Practical Guide to Challenging Homophobia in Schools*, February 1999, see accompanying video
76 *Loc cit*
77 *Daily Mail*, 2 March 1996
78 *Daily Mail*, July 1997
79 Mole, S, *Colours of the Rainbow*, Camden & Islington Community NHS Trust, 1995, page 80
80 *Ibid*, pages 86 and 87
81 *Ibid*, pages 135 - 138
82 *Daily Mail*, 10 October 1998
83 *Birmingham Post*, 10 October 1998
84 *Young People's Guide* Birmingham Health Authority/Birmingham Leisure and Community Services, 1998, page 6
85 *Ibid*, page 129
86 *Ibid*, page 128
87 *Ibid*, page 132
88 *Ibid*, page 86
89 *Ibid*, page 88
90 Islington Council, *Strength & Pride – Islington Libraries guide to books, music, videos & information*, 1996, pages 41-52
91 *Ibid* page 13
92 *Ibid* page 27
93 *Ibid* page 11
94 *Pink Paper*, 19 February 1999
95 *Pink Paper*, 30 April 1999
96 Job description for the post of Youth Worker (Temporary) PHASE, ref ED/PHASE/02, London Borough of Tower Hamlets
98 Conversation with Area Youth Co-ordinator, Georgette Wilson, 21 October 1999
99 Manchester City Council, Social & Urban Strategy Sub-Committee, report of the Chief Executive on Voluntary Organisations - Revenue Grants Programme 1999/2002, 15 March 1999, page 17
100 Taken from the charity's objects clause. Can be viewed at http://www.charity-commission.gov.uk/
101 http://www.peer-support.demon.co.uk/resources/out.htm
102 Hanrahatty, K, *Coming Out & Staying Out*, Peer Support Project, 1999
103 http://www.peer-support.demon.co.uk/
104 *Loc cit* See also Gay Times, May 1998, page 48
105 *Way out: working effectively with lesbian, gay and bisexual young people*, Education Department Youth Service, Oxfordshire County Council, Applicants' background information for a Part-time Youth-Worker Lesbian, Gay and Bi-sexual Group. As advertised in *Pink Paper* 11 December 1998
106 *Loc cit*
107 *Pink Paper* 11 December 1998
108 *Selection Criteria*, Education Department Youth Service, Oxfordshire County Council, Applicants' background information for a Part-time Youth-Worker Lesbian, Gay and Bi-sexual Group. As advertised in *Pink Paper* 11 December 1998
109 *Way out: working effectively with lesbian, gay and bisexual young people*, Education Department Youth Service, Oxfordshire County Council, Applicants' background information for a Part-time Youth-Worker Lesbian, Gay and Bi-sexual Group. As advertised in *Pink Paper* 11 December 1998
110 *Pink Paper*, 14 August 1998
111 *Pink Paper*, 18 June 1999
112 *Pink Paper* 9 July 1999.
113 *Pink Paper*, 4 September 1998
114 *Pink Paper*, 4 September 1998
115 *Pink Paper*, 19 February 1999
116 *Pink Paper*, 16 April 1999
117 *Pink Paper* 9 July 1999. Although advertised by the Council, the post is funded by Brent & Harrow Health Authority.
118 *It's Queer Up North Festival 1996* programme page 3
119 *Ibid*, page 13
120 *Ibid*, page 6
121 *Gay Times* July 1998 page 120
122 *Gay Times* April 1998 page 108
123 Glasgay! 1998 programme, page 3
124 *Ibid*, page 4
125 Glasgay! *Report On The 1998 Festival*, para 4.8
126 *Ibid*, table 3
127 Rights of Women Lesbian Custody Group, *Lesbian Mother's Legal Handbook*, The Women's Press, 1986, page 84
128 *Ibid*, page 88
129 Rights Of Women *Annual Review 1997-1998*
130 See library catalogue at http://webpac.camcnty.gov.uk/cam.html
131 See library catalogue at http://library.southampton.gov.uk/
132 See library catalogue at: http://www.buckscc.gov.uk/clink_for_pcat.htm
133 Leicester Lesbian, Gay and Bisexual Centre *Annual Report* 1997 - 1998. The centre also received £15,654 from the National Lottery.
134 Leicester Lesbian, Gay and Bisexual Centre *Annual Report* 1997 - 1998.
135 Bösche, S, *Jenny lives with Eric and Martin*, Gay Men's Press, 1983
136 See library catalogue for Hertfordshire libraries at http://hertslib.hertscc.gov.uk
137 *Gay Times* July 1999, pages 53-54
138 See library catalogue for Gloucestershire at http://opac.gloscc.gov.uk/www-bin/www_talis
139 Elliot K, *Zack's Story - Growing Up with Same-Sex Parents*, Lerner Publications, 1996
140 Lambeth, Southwark & Lewisham Health Authority, *Annual Report, AIDS (Control) Act 1987, HIV/AIDS and Related Services 1997/98 and Developments Commissioned for 1998/99*, Directorate of Health Policy and Public Health, March 1999, page 74, Table C.1
141 Lambeth, Southwark & Lewisham Health Authority, *Annual Report, AIDS (Control) Act 1987, HIV/AIDS and Related Services 1997/98 and Developments Commissioned for 1998/99*, Directorate of Health Policy and Public Health, March 1999, page 76, Table C.3
142 *Ibid*, page 78
143 www.palace.org.uk/leaflets/cruising.html
144 The Healthy Gay Living Centre (formerly the Lads Project), *Income and Expenditure Account* Year ended 31st March 1998